# Lost

## Written by Roger Cook

## CONTENTS

Endangered Tribes.............................. 2
Tribes of Africa
    The San ......................................... 4
    The Pygmy .................................... 6
Tribes of Asia
    The Khanty ................................. 8
Tribes of the Americas
    The Innu ..................................... 10
    The Awá ..................................... 12
Tribes of Australia
    The Aborigine ........................ 14
Lost Tribes......................................... 16
Index.................................................... 17

# Endangered Tribes

Today, scientists believe that there are as many as six and a half billion people living on the earth. With so many people, it is hard to believe that there are tribes in danger of becoming lost forever.

These endangered tribes can be found all over the world, in Africa, Asia, Australia, Europe and the Americas. Most have survived for hundreds of thousands of years, often living alone in areas far from cities and other people.

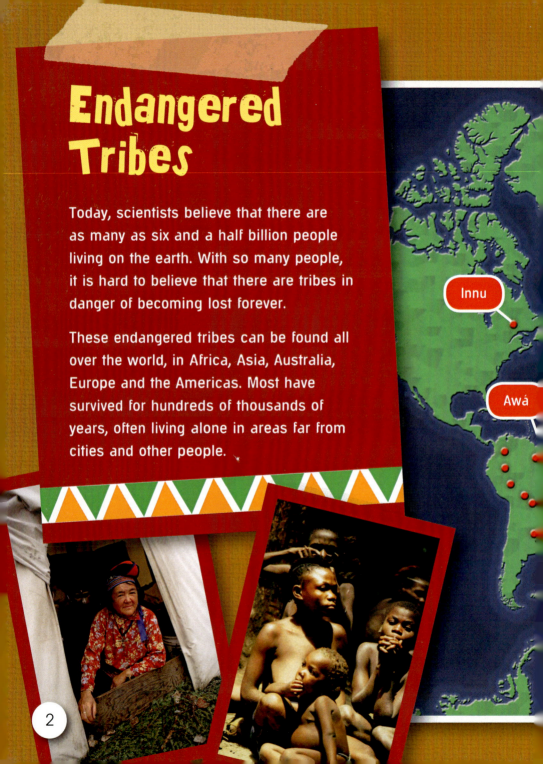

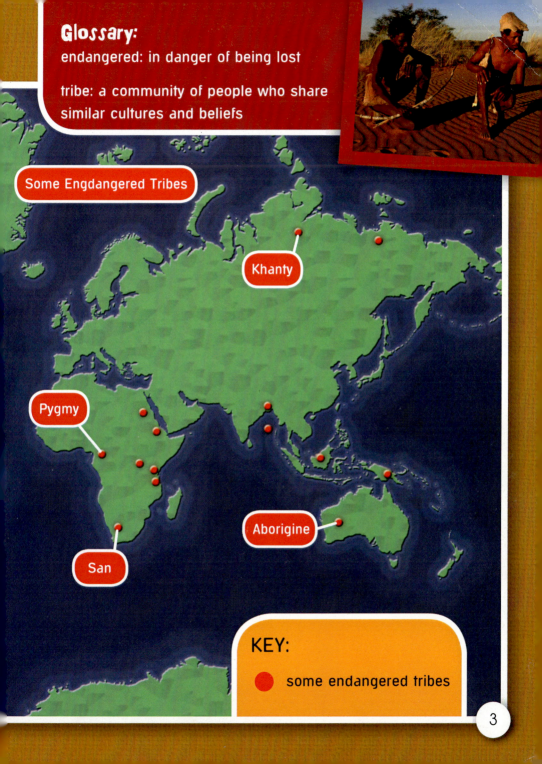

# Tribes of Africa

In Africa, there are many endangered tribes of people, including:
- the San
- the Maasai
- the Nuba
- the Pygmies
- the Ogiek.

## The San

One of the oldest tribes in Africa is the San. They have survived for more than 20 thousand years all over Africa. Some people call the San, Bushmen.

| San | Population | Approx 83,000 |

Most of the San live in the very hot, dry Kalahari Desert. Water and food is hard to find here, but the San are experts at finding and storing food and water. They are also very good at hunting and tracking animals. They can tell how big an animal is, how old it is, and how old the tracks are, just by looking at them.

Many years ago, the San would paint rock art on the walls of caves. Today, they no longer paint rock art, but they still make jewellery, bows and arrows, and musical instruments like their ancestors made.

In the past there were many San. But disease, war, and the first European people who sailed to Africa killed many.

Now there are only a few San left. Their biggest dangers are disease, modern life, governments and big business. The San are slowly losing their traditions as they get forced to move into the big cities. Mining companies looking for diamonds are also forcing them from their land.

If the San cannot return to their land, their traditions will be lost forever, and many of them will die.

Botswana

the San live here

**Fact Box:**
Scientists often call the San "the first people" because they were the very first people of Africa.

## The Pygmy

Until a few hundred years ago, nobody knew that the Pygmy even existed.

But like the San, the pygmies have survived in central and West Africa for thousands of years.

| Pygmy | Population | Approx 250,000 |

The Pygmy live deep in the rainforests in small groups. Their way of life and traditions have stayed unchanged for many years. The men hunt with bows and arrows and blowpipes that they make, and the women fish and collect fruit. The Pygmy know a lot about the forest and its plants and animals. They also know how to find their way around the dense, thick forest.

Scientists believe they can learn a lot from the Pygmy. Many plants and animals of the rainforest have not yet been discovered. The medicine men of the tribes may hold the key to curing many of the world's diseases.

### Fact Box:
There are many different Pygmy tribes and they speak different languages.

the Pygmy live here

logging in Central Africa

In the past, thousands of pygmy have died – and still die today – because of war and disease. Their forest home is disappearing as governments and big companies chop up the forests for farming and logging.

The pygmy believe that the forest is their only home. If they are forced to leave the forest or if the forest dies, they believe they will die, too.

# Tribes of Asia

There are many tribes in Asia that are also in danger of becoming lost forever. Some of these tribes are:

- the Khanty
- the Jarawa
- the Wanniyala-Aetto
- the Papuan tribes, and many others.

| Khanty | Population | Approx 23,000 |

## The Khanty

The Khanty are one of the world's oldest tribal groups. They live in the forests along the River Ob where the weather is very cold.

Like their ancestors, the Khanty herd reindeer, hunt and fish, and gather berries. They are nomads, moving from place to place, following the reindeer. The reindeer are very important to them, as they provide much needed food and skins for clothing and tents.

About 70 years ago, the government of Russia took much of the land away from the Khanty. They could not herd their reindeer. Many were forced to move to farms. Khanty children were also taken away from their parents and sent away.

Today, they face new dangers from big oil and gas companies. Oil spills have polluted the grasslands and the rivers, killing their reindeer and the fish. Many Khanty have been forced to move off their land and into villages.

# Tribes Of The Americas

The Americas are made up of North and South America, and there are nearly 886 million people living in its many countries. Some tribes that can be found living there are:

- the Innu
- the Inuit
- the Awá
- the Makuxi.

| The Innu | Population | Approx 18,000 |

## The Innu

The Innu were nomads. They lived in a very cold part of Canada, surrounded by forests, lakes and rivers. They would fish, gather berries, and hunt animals like bear, deer and caribou. The Innu used the caribou for food, tools, weapons and skins to make clothes and tents.

They lived like this for thousands of years, until a few hundred years ago. When the first Europeans arrived in Canada, they brought diseases that killed many Innu. Then, in the late 1950's, the government forced the Innu to move from their land to make way for roads, dams, mining and logging.

Today, most Innu practise very little of their old traditions, although some still hunt and fish. Their land is their history and their future, and without it, the Innu cannot survive as a tribe.

**Glossary:**
Nomad: people who have no permanent home

Canada

the Innu live here

**Fact Box:**
Many people get the Innu confused with the Inuit. They are two different tribes, but both are endangered.

# The Awá

| The Awá | Population | Approx 300 |
|---|---|---|

The Awá are nomads who live in the Amazon jungle in Brazil. They live in temporary shelters made out of leaves, which they leave behind in their search for food. As they travel, they keep the ashes from their fires alive, so they can have fire at their new shelter. Everything the Awá need to survive is in the jungle. Their food, water, clothing and weapons all come from plants and animals found in the jungle.

Today, only 300 Awá are left. The jungle they once knew is slowly being destroyed by farming and logging, making it difficult for them to survive. Disease, farmers and loggers have also killed many of them.

The Awá are a tribe in danger of becoming lost forever.

# Tribes Of Australia

When Australia was first discovered by Europeans, a tribe of people were found who had already been living there for thousands of years.

| Aborigine | Population | Approx 250,000 |

## The Aborigine

Scientists believe that the Aborigine have lived in Australia for more than 40,000 years, and their population was once as many as a million people. They lived in groups or clans, each with their own language and in their own area.

Some Aborigine clans lived near the sea. They farmed, fished and kept animals. Other clans lived more inland, in the bush and desert. The Aborigine survived by hunting and gathering, and, just like the San of Africa, they were very skilled at finding water.

**Fact Box:**
The Aborigine were good at arts and crafts, like painting, and making weapons and musical instruments.
The word Aborigine means "the first people" or "the people who were here from the beginning".

the Aborigine live here

When the first Europeans arrived in Australia, they brought many diseases that killed thousands of Aborigine. Many were also killed, and their land was taken away from them. Women and children were kidnapped and sent away to live in cities, never to see their families again.

Today, the Aborigine still face many problems. They are still fighting to get their land back and many of their traditions have been lost.

# Lost Tribes

The way of life for these endangered tribes has been the same for centuries. We have so much to learn from them and about them. For many, time is running out. For some tribes it is already too late.

If we continue to take their land and destroy their homes, they will soon be gone.

Pygmy outside their huts

# Index

African tribes ................................................. 2, 4
    Pygmies ........................................... 4, 6-7
    San ..................................................... 4-5
American tribes ........................................... 2, 10
    Awá ................................................... 10, 12
    Innu ........................................................ 10
Asian tribes .................................................... 2, 8
    Khanty ........................................................ 8
Australian tribes .......................................... 2, 14
    Aborigine ............................................. 14-15
companies ......................................... 5, 7, 8, 10
disease ........................................ 5, 7, 10, 12, 15
government ............................................ 5, 7, 8
groups ...................................................... 6, 8, 14
nomads ......................................................... 8, 10
traditions ............................................. 5, 6, 10, 15
war ................................................................. 5, 7

# Explanations

**Lost Tribes** is an **Explanation**.

An explanation explains **how** or **why** things happen.

An explanation has a topic:

> **Lost Tribes**

An explanation has headings:

> **Endangered Tribes**

> **Tribes of Africa**

> **The San**

Some information is put under headings:

### THE SAN

There are few San because of:
- disease
- government
- big business.

Information can be shown in other ways. This explanation has...

Labels    Bullet Points
    Captions    Photographs

Maps

# Guide Notes

**Title:** Lost Tribes
**Stage:** Fluency

**Text Form:** Informational Explanation
**Approach:** Guided Reading
**Processes:** Thinking Critically, Exploring Language, Processing Information
**Written and Visual Focus:** Contents Page, Bullet Points, Captions, Labels, Maps, Index

## THINKING CRITICALLY
(sample questions)
**Before Reading – Establishing Prior Knowledge**
- What do you know about lost tribes?

**Visualising the Text Content**
- What might you expect to see in this book?
- What form of writing do you think will be used by the author?

Look at the contents page and index. Encourage the students to think about the information and make predictions about the text content.

**After Reading – Interpretation**
- Why do you think some tribes have become endangered?
- Do you think there are things we could learn from these endangered tribes? Why do you think that?
- What do you think are some of the reasons for tribes becoming endangered?
- Do you think it is important to save endangered tribes? Why or why not?
- What things can we do to save endangered tribes? Why do you think that?
- What do you know about lost tribes that you didn't know before?
- What in the book helped you understand the information?
- What questions do you have after reading the text?

## EXPLORING LANGUAGE

### Terminology
Photograph credits, index, contents page, imprint information, ISBN number